SKETCH

Book

This book belongs to:

Made in the USA
Las Vegas, NV
06 December 2024

13471086R10063